Jaguars
For Kids

Amazing Animal Books
For Young Readers

By
Rachel Smith

Mendon Cottage Books
JD-Biz Corp Publishing

Read More Amazing Animal Books

Purchase at Amazon.com

Table of Contents

Introduction

The jaguar is one of the most beautiful cats in existence. With its spotted coat and its piercing eyes, it's captured the imagination of many an artist or storyteller.

The third biggest cat in the world, the jaguar is a mass of deadly muscle. It's the biggest predator in South America, and the symbol of strength in Aztec culture.

There isn't much about the jaguar that's boring. Like the tiger and the lion, they attract the attention of much of humanity.

What is a jaguar?

The jaguar is known as the Panthera Onca. Panthera is the family that most big cats belong to, such as leopards, panthers, lions, and tigers, among others.

A jaguar

Jaguars are the only Panthera family member in South America. They are amazing predators, with very strong jaws. Their jaws are strong even compared to other big cats, and can bite through reptile's shells.

The name jaguar actually comes to us from a native word for the jaguar. It's a Tupinamba word, the Tupinamba language being a trading language. It was then crossed over into Spanish and Portuguese as jaguar.

The jaguar is most close to the leopard in appearance. They both have spots, and a similar background coat color, but that's where a lot of the similarities end. The jaguar is much more muscular and sturdily built than the leopard. It's also larger than the leopard.

They are not quite as big as lions and tigers, as noted before. The jaguar is the third largest cat in the world, not counting extinct cats.

They are very muscular, and have short, thick legs compared to other cats. It is incredibly well colored and patterned for its environment; the spots covering its body are called dapples, or rosettes.

Most jaguars are yellow and black, but there are some that end up entirely black. These are called melanistic jaguars. Unlike some species that end up having completely black or completely white animals through mutation, it seems the melanistic gene is far more common than a mutation, and it is just normal. It doesn't make the melanistic jaguars more likely to die, as far as scientists can tell, unlike albinism, which is where the animal is completely white due to lack of coloring in their skin and such.

Melanistic jaguars are also known as black panthers. This is not a separate species, however. Black panther is just the name for both melanistic jaguars and melanistic leopards.

Jaguars can cross-breed with lions, tigers, and leopards. A lot of the time, such breedings are by mistake, but it has been shown that some of these hybrids are actually fertile, which is not always the case when two species can cross-breed.

Once, a man tried to pass off a jaguar-leopard hybrid as a new animal. This was in 1900, so he mostly succeeded thanks to people not knowing a lot about either animal.

One interesting case of this cross-breeding is the jaglion cubs given birth to by the lioness Lola in the Bear Creek Wildlife Sanctuary in Canada. The babies were sired by a black jaguar named Diablo. In this case, Lola and Diablo had been raised together and were inseparable; they ended up having the cubs due to this close bond.

One of the cubs, Tsunami, is a spotted jaglion, whereas the other cub, Jahzara, is melanistic like her father.

The tiguar or the jagger, which are both names for tiger and jaguar hybrids, have not been proven to exist, though there have been reports of such animals existing.

Interestingly, the jaguar's size tends to vary depending on where it lives. Some jaguars are huge compared to jaguars in other areas.

Jaguars are extremely good at things like climbing, swimming, and crawling. It is incredibly strong, and it depends on being able to do these things to help it hunt.

They are carnivores, meaning that they require meat to survive. A jaguar cannot be a 'vegetarian', as they will undoubtedly die. Like cats the world over, their whole system is designed to live off of meat.

How do jaguars act?

Jaguars have a lot of behavior that fascinates humans. To begin with, the jaguar reproductive cycle is one that interests many zoologists. Zoologists are people who study animals.

A melanistic jaguar, notice that you can see its rosettes, or spots.

Jaguars mate all the year round. They don't have a mating season like some animals, though it seems like the amount of prey available makes a difference. If there is more food to eat, then the jaguars are more likely to try to mate.

A female jaguar lets males know she is ready to mate by peeing on certain areas within her territory and by making loud noises. She is trying to attract males, since jaguars are solitary and don't roam in packs or anything like that. The male would not immediately know she wants to mate, since they don't live near each other.

Jaguars mate once, and then the male leaves. The female is left to care for the cubs by herself, not unlike tigers. In fact, the male has nothing to do with the cubs at all, and the mother prefers all males gone. Why? Because, again like the tiger, a male who happens upon cubs will probably kill them.

The reason a jaguar does this, presumably, is to prevent competition. Same with the tiger. It doesn't want to have other males' cubs in its area, because that means another male is succeeding.

You might think, isn't there plenty to go around? Why on earth would a male kill cubs?

But the fact is that this has long been a part of many of the big cats' ways of living, and it will probably never change, no matter how abundant food and territory are. And they aren't very abundant right now anyway.

The cubs are born blind. They are able to see after about two weeks. The mother carries them for around three months, a lot shorter than a human mom, who must carry her baby, or babies, for about nine months.

The mother takes care of her cubs; typically, she has anywhere from one to four cubs, though two is the most common number. The cubs nurse for about three months, and then they are weaned. Weaned means that they are taught to eat solid food and not rely on their mother's milk anymore.

At six months, they join their mother on her hunts. By one or two years, the jaguar cubs are grown up, and they leave and establish their own territory. Males typically end up a bit nomadic, which means that they wander a lot with no fixed home. They have to jostle their way into territory among older males, and this is no easy feat. However, most accomplish it, since there is little other option.

The reason that the males have a harder time is that males' territory is different from females' territory. For one thing, the females have smaller territories, and they don't mind overlapping with each other. Males, on the other hand, have twice the size and will absolutely not overlap with other males.

Both genders of jaguars mark their territory with scrapes, pee, and poop. This leaves a scent that warns other jaguars that this territory is taken.

Males don't mind having females within their territory. In fact, most fights are about either territory, or competing for mates. But the jaguar is not actually a very aggressive creature against its own kind. Instead, they tend to try to avoid fights.

Often, instead of fighting, they will just roar at each other. This does not sound all that much like the roaring of other big cats; instead, it can sound more like coughing. Often, this roar will be used to warn other males away, and the other male may sound counter-roars back. Most of the time, this doesn't lead to a fight.

Jaguars are solitary creatures. This means they prefer to be alone; the only grouping that is almost ever seen in the wild is the grouping of mother and cubs.

Jaguars prefer to hunt big animals, but often have to make do with smaller prey. The American tropics have far fewer large prey than Old World habitats for big cats. Animals a jaguar might hunt include caimans, deer, peccaries, tapir, capybaras, dogs, and zorros. It will also eat smaller prey such as turtles, birds, mice, frogs, armadillos, and other small creatures.

The jaguar consumes at least eighty-seven other species.

Jaguars have specific ways of killing their prey. First is the most typical for a big cat, which is lunging for the throat and sinking their teeth in. An animal bitten on the neck will usually die quite quickly.

Another way, which seems to be unique to the jaguar, is to break open their skull with their jaws. This is done by biting between the ears, and not a little nip, but fully sinking the jaws in. Some scientists believe this is something that the jaguar learned how to do so that it could do this to turtle shells. It does, in fact, hunt even enormous leatherback turtles, which weigh over three hundred and eighty kilograms.

With horses, which it sometimes hunts, it will jump on its back, put one paw on the nape of the neck, and one paw on the muzzle; then it will twist, and dislocate the neck of the horse. Then it drags it away to eat it.

Dogs, which it sometimes hunts, aren't usually even bitten in this way. Because dogs are so much smaller and weaker, they usually can just hit them with their paw and kill them.

Jaguars do not chase down their prey, unlike other big cats. Instead, they sneak up on them and ambush them. The jaguar is considered to be the best at ambushing in the animal kingdom. Typically, it will drag its prey away after the attack, to more a secluded area, where it eats the chest and neck area, plus the lungs and heart, first.

Jaguars require a certain amount of meat a day, but in the wild they are much more erratic feeders. It's hard to bring down a big kill, and they definitely can't do it every day. So, oftentimes, they will simply gorge themselves on their kill, and then go without for a while.

Fortunately, jaguars are rarely interested in hunting humans. If they do, it's probably a very weak one, one that's old and toothless or wounded. They do this out of desperation.

They have been known to very rarely attack zookeepers, but that's only when the jaguar feels cornered and afraid.

Where did jaguars come from?

Jaguars originally come from the single ancestor of lions, tigers, leopards, snow leopards, and tigers. A very long time ago, it was just the one animal that would eventually evolve into all of these cats; then, it split again.

A mama and baby jaguars.

After it split for the first time, it split one more time on the side the jaguar was on, and then, with the ancestor of the leopard and the jaguar, it split one last time, and led to these two beautiful cats.

The thought is that the ancestors of the jaguar crossed Beringia around two million years ago. Beringia was a land bridge between

North America and Asia. This is because the single ancestor of these big cats was Asian, though, as we already know, the jaguar is the only one in the Americas, though mostly in South America.

Now, one key thing to know about Beringia is that having come over that way does not make the jaguar any less of a native South-and-Central American animal. It's evolved to be adapted to its environment, and while it might survive somewhere else, it's best suited to its home. It's been there for possibly millions of years, from its ancestor onwards.

So, the fact that its ancestor originated in Asia does not really affect whether or not it belongs in its current habitat.

As far as we know, humans originated in Africa, and that doesn't make us all African, after all.

The ancestor of the jaguar was actually bigger than today's jaguar. That's something that happened with mega fauna all over the world.

Mega fauna are basically giant animals. This refers to a specific period in Earth's history where many, many giant animals existed. In South America, animals such as the giant ground sloth, which was as big as a modern day elephant, roamed amid an abundant food source.

What made the big difference in size was there being more oxygen in the air. It was also a pretty fertile and even warm earth, more affected by greenhouse gases than today.

The moose is a modern day surviving mega fauna. Most of the mega fauna, however, died out when the ice age happened. Where there had once been a lot of food, there was no more to support such big animals. All over the world, these big animals died out, though not immediately. They couldn't evolve fast enough to adapt to a rapidly changing world, and so became extinct, as far as we know long before humans had anything to do with it.

So, jaguars are some of the lucky ones that were able to adapt.

Where do jaguars live?

Jaguars live in Central and South America. They are quite well known in their homeland, and for a long time, were revered by various native cultures as powerful beasts and other entities.

A black jaguar.

There are two countries in Central and South America that the jaguar has become extinct: El Salvador and Uruguay. Otherwise, it basically lives in most of the South America continent and in most of Central America. It does not live in the Caribbean Islands.

A chief area it can live is Mexico. This is mostly as far north as it goes, but that's not always the case. The United States of America is considered something of a habitat for it, as it has been spotted in the areas of Arizona, New Mexico, and Texas. Since these are the parts closest to Mexico, this makes sense.

However, the United States doesn't really have a stable population of jaguars. Instead, it's sort of scattered randomly and not really a set habitat. The number of jaguars spotted in Arizona, for example, could be counted on one hand. They've been there since the nineties at least.

The only way for the United States to end up with a stable population would be for there to be more protection for jaguars, as they are often a problem for livestock and therefore a target of the ranchers and farmers, and for them to have a connection with the Mexican jaguars, so that there's enough genetic diversity. This will probably not happen.

The jaguar actually used to live much farther north in America. Thousands of years ago, they ranged about a thousand kilometers higher than they do now, possibly even farther than that.

For example, fossils have been found as far north as Missouri, a mid-Western state.

As for actual habitat conditions, or how the area it lives in is, the jaguar tends to prefer rainforest, partially because their populations have been reduced in other areas, but they like dry grasslands, dry deciduous (deciduous means trees that drop their leaves yearly) forests, open wetlands, and many other areas. It does not like mountains, though.

What kind of jaguars are there?

The truth is, there are a number of subspecies of jaguars. There are three main subspecies: the 'main' subspecies, which is mostly the Amazonian jaguar, the Mexican jaguar, and the largest subspecies, which is less specific in which area it belongs to.

A male jaguar from Brazil.

Within the 'main' jaguar, there's the Peruvian jaguar, which is the kind that lives in Peru.

Then, within the Mexican jaguar, there are a number of subspecies. The Central American jaguar, which lives mostly near El Salvador (but no longer in it), the Arizonan jaguar, the jaguar that lives from Texas to part of Mexico, and the Goldman's jaguar, which lives in areas like Belize.

The largest subspecies has no other divisions, and simply lives in parts of Brazil, Argentina, and Paraguay.

If you were to go back in time, you would find a number of early jaguar-ancestors as well, but those are not as well known or defined as the current subspecies of jaguars.

The history of jaguars and humans

Jaguars have long inspired humans. The native cultures in the area, most notably in Mexico, developed entire mythologies and other beliefs around them.

A jaguar in a zoo.

This is very similar to the stuff that grew up in Europe about animals like wolves and then, as they discovered other lands, the lion, the tiger, and other such creatures they considered majestic and powerful. The lion, despite not even living in Europe, is in many coats of arms and is one of the animals that represents England, the other being the imaginary unicorn.

So, the jaguar, as a very powerful hunter in Central and South America, was bound to be a part of the cultures there. What we know the most about are mostly the cultural things that sprung up in Mexico and nearby areas.

One that wasn't Mexican was the jaguar cult that grew in the Andes. Also, jaguars were important parts of many cultures in those areas, seen as creatures representing power and strength.

The Olmecs, who came before the Aztecs and were gone by the time explorers reached this area, are known for having made rather 'were-jaguar' type of sculptures and figures. That is, like the werewolf, these figures had somewhat jaguar bodes and features, but also human features and often posture.

This was passed down into the Aztec culture, who were highly influenced by the Olmecs. The Maya and the Aztecs associated the jaguar with royalty and power. The jaguar was said to protect the royal family.

The Aztecs especially used this in the class of Jaguar Knights, also known as Jaguar Warriors. These men would wear jaguar pelts as clothes, because it was believed the power of the animal would be transferred to them.

One thing to understand about Aztec culture is that there was a huge focus on human sacrifice. There's nothing pretty about that, but it's the reality of the Aztec culture. They honestly believed they needed to sacrifice to their gods to keep the sun coming up and things like that.

So, when they went to war, it was rarely because they were fighting over something. Instead, it was because they needed more victims.

The only way to become a jaguar warrior was to capture, not kill, twelve enemies in two battles, one after the other. In these battles, it was seen as far better to capture than to kill, so that the captives could be sacrificed.

A jaguar warrior would be armed with a sort of sword called a macuahuitl, which was wooden and had sharp obsidian glass studded along its sides. They may also have fought with spears and other weapons.

Today, the jaguar still has a place of importance, though not quite of the mythological standards that it held back before the area was taken over by the Spanish and Portuguese.

For example, it's the national animal of Guyana, a small country in South America, and they use it in their coat of arms. Another example is how it's used on Brazilian bank notes.

Probably one of the most well-known brands of car is the Jaguar. This is a very expensive kind of car that took the name of the jaguar to sound very cool. It's a British brand, interestingly, another example of a company taking an 'exotic' thing from another country and using it.

Conclusion

So, jaguars are an interesting and mesmerizing animal. They are doing okay, even with the ways they've lost some of their habitat. And in native cultures, they will probably always be revered or respected.

The jaguar is a testament to the way an animal can adapt to its environment. It is a beautiful creature, but not one to be messed with.

Hopefully, the jaguar will continue its existence without having to worry too much about humans.

Author Bio

Rachel Smith is a young author who enjoys animals. Once, she had a rabbit who was very nervous, and chewed through her leash and tried to escape. She's also had several pet mice, who were the funniest little animals to watch. She lives in Ohio with her family and writes in her spare time.

Publisher

JD-Biz Corp

P O Box 374

Mendon, Utah 84325

http://www.jd-biz.com/

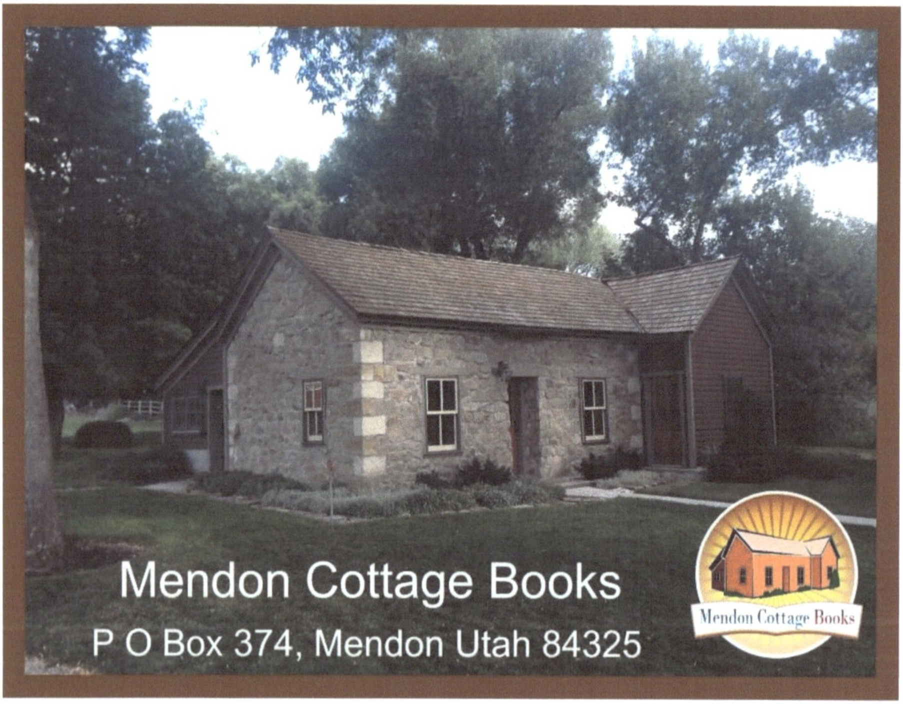

Mendon Cottage Books

P O Box 374, Mendon Utah 84325

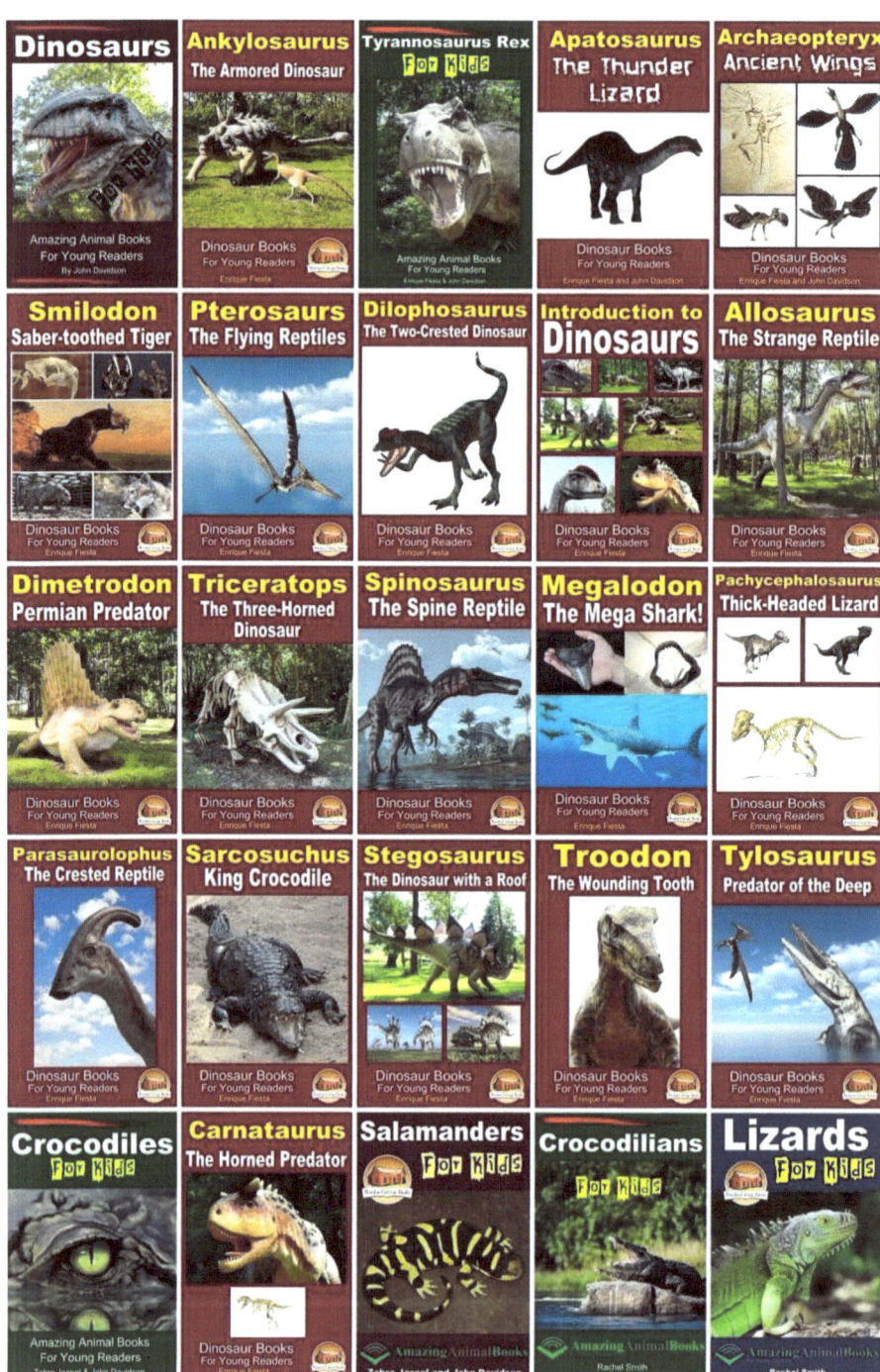

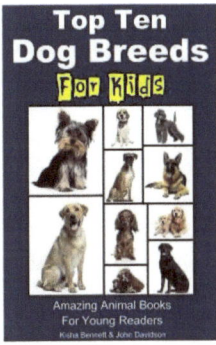

Top Ten Dog Breeds For Kids

Amazing Animal Books For Young Readers

German Shepherds

Dog Books for Kids
K. Bennett

Bulldogs

Dog Books for Kids
K. Bennett

Dachshund

Dog Books for Kids
K. Bennett

Labrador Retrievers

Poodles

Dog Books for Kids
K. Bennett

Dog Books for Kids
K. Bennett

Rottweilers

Dog Books for Kids
K. Bennett

Boxers

Dog Books for Kids
K. Bennett

Golden Retrievers

Dog Books for Kids
K. Bennett

Puppies

Dog Books For Kids

Amazing Animal Books
By John Davidson

Beagles

Dog Books for Kids
K. Bennett

Yorkshire Terriers

Dog Books for Kids
K. Bennett

Dogs Top Ten Dog Breeds For Kids

Amazing Animal Books For Young Readers
Zahra Jazeel & John Davidson

Cats For Kids

Amazing Animal Books For Young Readers
K. Bennett & John Davidson

Foxes For Kids

Amazing Animal Books For Young Readers
Zahra Jazeel & John Davidson

Wolves For Kids

Amazing Animal Books For Young Readers
By John Davidson and Virginia Fidler

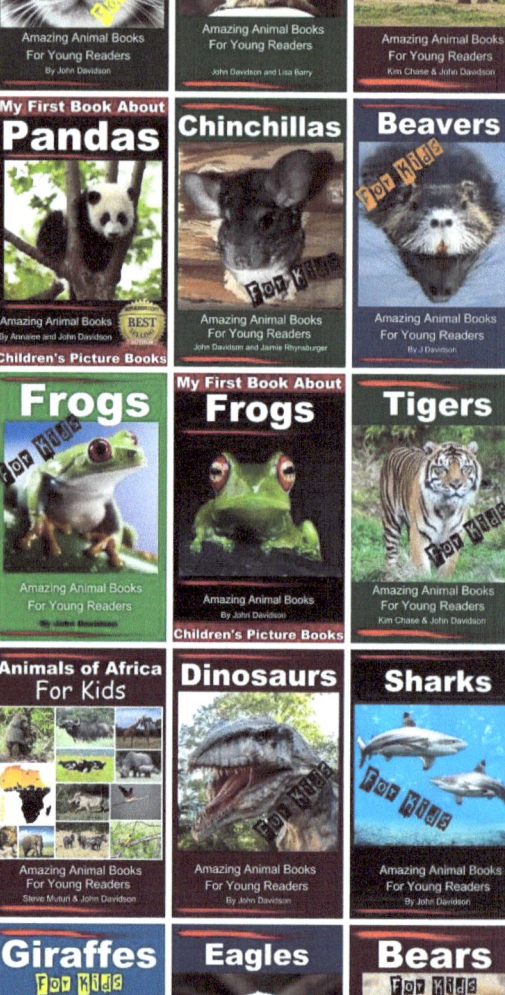